Two-part

Let's Sing!

Volume Two

Five Diverse Selections
for the School Year

HERITAGE
MUSIC PRESS

Compiled by: Mark Jauss, Jr.
Cover Art: Patti Jeffers
Engraver: Sandra R. Wagner

ISBN: 978-0-7877-6640-5

© 2019 Heritage Music Press, a division of The Lorenz Corporation.
All rights reserved. Printed in the U.S.A.

C000163451

Foreword

As a one-stop-shopping, budget-stretching collection, *Let's Sing!* brings together ten diverse Two-part selections in two volumes for use throughout the school year. You'll find easily learned, tried-and-true titles for Christmas and Halloween, and as well as Patriotic music, Spirituals, Multicultural music, and General-use works for any occasion, all written by composers and arrangers who are well-known for consistently creating effective music for the developing voice – Mark Burrows, Greg Gilpin, Victor C. Johnson, and Douglas E. Wagner, just to name a few.

An Accompaniment CD is also available, not only as an aid in rehearsals, but also for performance use, if necessary. Several of the selections have orchestrated tracks.

We have no doubt that this practical, confidence-building two-volume set will be a go-to library resource for years to come, as it helps to bring out the very best from your young singers.

So with deep breaths, tall vowels, and crisp consonants …

Let's Sing!

– The Publisher

Contents

Also available:
45/1637H   Volume One
99/3999H   Accompaniment CD (for both Volumes)

Permission-to-Reproduce Notice

Permission to photocopy the choral scores included in this collection is hereby granted to one teacher, as part of the purchase price. This permission may not be transferred, sold, or given to any additional or subsequent user of this product. Thank you for respecting copyright laws.

Kye Kye Kule

Two-part and Piano with Percussion and optional Descant

Traditional West African Folk Song
Arranged by **Mark Burrows**

Continue four bar percussion pattern through measure 72,
following the dynamics of the piano part.

Duration: approx. 1:40

© 2017 Heritage Music Press, a division of The Lorenz Corporation. All rights reserved. Printed in U.S.A.
Unauthorized reproduction of this publication is a criminal offense subject to prosecution.
Copying this music is illegal. A license from CCLI or OneLicense does not grant permission to copy.

www.lorenz.com

6

long._____ You have a song.

I Kye-kye ko - fi - sa. Kye-kye ku - la - la.

II Kye-kye ko - fi - sa.

(end Descant)

Come join a - long._____

I Ko - fi - sa - lan - ga.

II Kye-kye ku - la - la. Ko - fi - sa - lan - ga.

Dedicated to the 2010–2011 Rising Starr Middle School Chorus, Fayetteville, GA

All on a Silent Night

Two-part and Piano with optional Cello*

Words and Music by
Becki Slagle Mayo
Incorporating *Silent Night*

Duration: approx. 2:55

*Cello part is available as a free download. Visit www.lorenz.com, search "15/2915H",
and click on the item image.

Also available: SATB (15/3336H); Three-part Mixed (15/3651H); SSA (15/3443H); TTB (15/3656H).

© 2012 Heritage Music Press, a division of The Lorenz Corporation. All rights reserved. Printed in U.S.A.
Unauthorized reproduction of this publication is a criminal offense subject to prosecution.
Copying this music is illegal. A license from CCLI or OneLicense does not grant permission to copy.

www.lorenz.com

LT

14

45/1638H-14

16

*Higher notes preferred, if range permits.

for the SW Missouri District 11 Elementary Honor Choir,
premiered at the SWMMEA Convention March 7, 2015 at Carthage, Missouri
Mark Hayes, Conductor

Cold Snap

Two-part and Piano

Deborah Craig-Claar

Mark Hayes

Duration: approx. 2:15

Choreography suggestions are available as a free download. Visit www.lorenz.com, search "15/3275H", and click on the item image.

© 2016 Heritage Music Press, a division of The Lorenz Corporation. All rights reserved. Printed in U.S.A.
Unauthorized reproduction of this publication is a criminal offense subject to prosecution.
Copying this music is illegal. A license from CCLI or OneLicense does not grant permission to copy.

20

lakes start to freeze. Time to wave good-bye to fall.

lakes start to freeze. Time to wave good-bye to fall, to fall.

Finger snaps

Old Man Win-ter's come to call with a cold—— snap,

Old Man Win-ter's come to call with a cold—— snap,

with a cold—— snap!

with a cold—— snap!

North winds are blow-ing and chill-ing the air. Muf-flers and mit-tens are

Chill-ing the air.

what we all wear. Bet-ter go 'n' buy sup-plies.

Bet-ter go 'n' buy, bet-ter buy sup-plies.

Now's the time to win-ter-ize for a cold snap,

Now's the time to win-ter-ize for a cold snap,

* Hold nose and speak in a nasal voice.

*Hold hands at throat and speak in a high, raspy voice.
**Make coughing and sneezing sounds in rhythm.

*All shiver and say "Brrr!" in rhythm.

In Paradisum

Two-part and Piano

Gabriel Fauré
from *Requiem* (Opus 48)
Arranged by **Geoffrey Edwards**

Duration: approx. 3:00

© 2017 Heritage Music Press, a division of The Lorenz Corporation. All rights reserved. Printed in U.S.A.
Unauthorized reproduction of this publication is a criminal offense subject to prosecution.
Copying this music is illegal. A license from CCLI or OneLicense does not grant permission to copy.
www.lorenz.com

sw

28

45/1638H-28

All Night, All Day *with*
My Lord, What a Morning

Two-part and Piano

Traditional African-American Spirituals
Arranged by **Russell Robinson**

Duration: approx. 3:40

© 2018 Heritage Music Press, a division of The Lorenz Corporation. All rights reserved. Printed in U.S.A.
Unauthorized reproduction of this publication is a criminal offense subject to prosecution.
Copying this music is illegal. A license from CCLI or OneLicense does not grant permission to copy.

www.lorenz.com

SW

42

Other Popular Two-part Titles

General
15/2654H	Bonse Aba – Victor C. Johnson
15/1081H	Inscription of Hope – Z. Randall Stroope
15/2384H	She Sings ... – Amy F. Bernon
H5890	Something Told the Wild Geese – Sherri Porterfield
15/2812H	Whisper! – Greg Gilpin

Christmas
15/2489H	A La Nanita Nana – Ruth Elaine Schram
15/2179H	African Noel – Victor C. Johnson
15/2916H	Duérmete (The Angels' Lullaby) – Victor C. Johnson
15/2906H	I See a Star – Greg Gilpin
15/1286H	Sing for Joy – Linda Spevacek

Christmas (Secular)
15/2307H	A Bell Carol – Linda Spevacek
15/1537H	Christmas ... In About Three Minutes – Mark Weston
15/3124H	A Jolly, Jingling Christmas Medley – Greg Gilpin
15/2976H	A Merry, Merry Christmas to You! – Douglas E. Wagner
15/2497H	The Night Before Christmas – Mark Weston

Hanukkah
15/2694H	Hanerot Halalu (Light the Candles) – Becki Slagle Mayo
15/2569H	A Hanukkah Remembrance – Victor C. Johnson
15/3390H	Hanukkah, Season of Joy! – Douglas E. Wagner
15/1792H	Hanukkah Shalom – Ruth Elaine Schram
15/2691H	It's a Hanukkah Song (in a Major Key!) – Mark Burrows

(Continued on next page)

Spiritual

15/1348H	Joshua Fit the Battle of Jericho – Brad Printz
15/3488H	Keep Your Lamps! – Victor C. Johnson
HV159	Moses, Now Your People Are Free – Cynthia Gray
15/2932H	Swing Down, Ezekiel! – Greg Gilpin
15/1248H	Wade in the Water – Brad Printz

Multicultural

15/1534H	Ahrirang – Brad Printz
15/3205H	Artza Alinu – Russell Robinson
15/3388H	Bwana Awabariki *with* Kum Ba Ya – Mark Weston
15/3231H	Dide ta Deo – Mark Weston
15/1824H	Zum Gali Gali – Greg Giplin

Patriotic

15/1655H	I Hear America Singing – André J. Thomas
15/2659H	Let Freedom Ring! – Jerry Estes
15/1625H	A Patriotic Salute – Linda Spevacek
15/3399H	Singing Freedom's Song – Natalie Sleeth
15/1848H	Woke Up This Morning – Cynthia Gray

Various and Sundry

15/1926H	Antonio – Eugene Butler
15/2904H	Busy, Busy Bumblebee – Greg Gilpin
15/1548H	Chumbara – Dave and Jean Perry
15/2572H	Duct Tape (Materia Potens et Adhaesiva) – Mark Burrows
15/2936H	I've Been Good – Phyllis Wolfe White
H5891	I've Lost My Homework – Marta Keen
15/3423H	Jabberwocky – Mark Burrows
HV191	New Shoes Blues – Roger Lentz
15/2878H	Possum Gonna Play ... – Vijay Singh
15/2861H	Stodola Pumpa – Mark Weston